Forward

Jesus is said to have told his followers, *"Ask and ye shall receive,"* I believe he was telling us we have to ask. For in this place of "free will," our prayers cannot be answered unless they are first conveyed.

In one of the darkest times of my life, as I pleaded to God for understanding, I clearly heard what I have come to know as the voice of Spirit. *"Are you ready now,"* I was asked.

In order to discern this voice, I began to write down that which I was perceiving. To my amazement, even after much soul searching and scrutiny I came to understand that they come from that of the Christ consciousness; that of love and compassion, truth and honor.

The messages I have shared in this book come from this state of consciousness, offered to you in Love and Light as gift from Spirit. There is no coincidence that you are holding this book in your hands right now. So if it is your will, then ask that through God's grace a message be imparted unto you that is for your highest good.

State that you will not accept anything unto yourself that is not of God's Love and Light. Then relax and breathe in the loving presence of divine grace, letting go any other thoughts. When you are ready, randomly open the book. You will undoubtedly be drawn to a message that will speak directly to your situation.

Spirit says, *"Take from these messages only that which truly speaks to your heart. And know that what is shared with you comes in and of the Light.*

In Love and Light

Whisperings

✦　　✦

✦

Messages conveyed by:

S. E. Kuenzel

Author's website and contact information at:
www.OneInLoveAndLight.com

Cover design by: www.MusicCityDesign.com

Acknowledgements

While walking this great path into Love and Light, there have been so many wonderful souls I have encountered. I would simply like to say thank you to all of you in spirit and in the physical world. It is an honor and privilege to walk beside you. . .

Blessings of Love and Light to all

S. E. Kuenzel

Introduction

In this turbulent time of change and transformation, so many are asking, why does life have to be so challenging; why disease, why famine, why poverty, why war, why am I alone? Our plight on this Earth begs the question, where is this divine and loving presence we innately call to?

These questions weighed heavily on my mind as I helplessly witnessed a beautiful young loved one slowly taken by leukemia. It was while questioning, "Where is God?" that from the silence of seemingly unanswered prayers I heard his messenger. *"Are you ready now,"* I was asked. The voice was so clear, so undeniably that of Spirit and yet, as I think most of us would do, I couldn't help but wonder, was it God, was it an angel, or something else?

For weeks I pondered both the question and its origin, fearful of embracing that which was so unknown, and yet something from within said, *"Have courage and move forward in faith. This is your calling."*

Weeks passed while I sat idle, uncertain as to the course to choose. Then one day it hit me; the thought that moving forward into that unknown really wasn't any scarier than sitting still. Cautiously and with condition, I answered. "Yes, I am ready. I'm ready to embrace this calling I feel from within me, but only in the vein of love and peace, with honor and dignity, and in the spirit of the Christ consciousness."

It was there that my journey began, one that swiftly moved me into the heart of what I call a spiritual awakening. Long forgotten gifts of clairvoyance began emerging into the forefront of my awareness. As if God had lifted a veil, I began having visions and also found that not only was I aware of those in spirit, but I was also hearing their directives.

Still I couldn't help being skeptical of that which I was perceiving, so I began recording their guidance in a journal. It was only then that it became clear that not only was I connecting with loved ones who had passed but with those I came to understand were spirit guides, angels and ascended masters.

After several years of recording their guidance, one evening as I read a message for a friend, synchronicity opened a door. "It sounds like the message was written just for me," she said. The steering of the universe didn't end there. Over the course of the next several months there were nearly a dozen people for whom I read that made the same exact comment. That's when I knew that the messages were meant to be shared.

By the grace of God, that which is conveyed in this book was provided by those who resonate with the vibration of Love and Light. They come from many spheres of spiritual consciousness, including ascended masters, angels, and Archangels. I have chosen to refer to them collectively as *Spirit*.

When one reads from their messages, it becomes obvious that they are not contrary to any religion, nor are they postulating a religion. They are merely supplemental revelations spoken through divine grace in order that we might understand a little bit more about divine design, about karma and the power each of us holds in our words, deeds and actions. They offer enlightening information about why life is, and how we can and will affect our own future collectively and individually as evolving spirits.

Through the choices we make in our words, deeds and actions, we are constantly demonstrating that which we have learned through our lessons regarding love and compassion, respect and honor, to name a few. And through these demonstrations we create that which we still have a need to be tempered in. We know it as karma, the cause and effect aspect of that which we have chosen.

In so making these choices, we create the karma that will shape the future lessons of this life as well as the ones to come. *"You will reap that which you sow," the great master Jesus said.* Through your choices, the future is yours to sow. You can create and engage the energy of Love and Light, or you can wallow in the oppressive energy of fear and negativity. The question is, in every moment that comes before you, which will you choose?

As was mentioned in the forward, the messages I have shared in this book are offered to you in Love and Light as gift from Spirit. If it is your will to ask, hold it in your hands and ask that through God's grace a message be imparted unto you that comes in and of Love and Light for your highest good.

State that you will not accept anything unto yourself that is not of God's Love and Light. Then relax and breathe in the loving presence of divine grace, letting go any other thoughts. When you are ready, randomly open the book. You will undoubtedly be drawn to a message that will speak directly to your situation.

It is my sincere desire that the messages contained within will bring only that which will serve your highest good, and help you realize what a positive force you can be if you choose to be. May you prosper in peace, love and harmony, and may the divine design of your life reveal itself through the wonderful attributes of God's grace.

In Love and Light,

S. E. Kuenzel

*Scott Elliott - Kuenzel (**Kenzel**)*

The divine is waiting for you to impart words of commitment unto your journey. As you speak these words, you are creating a new chapter of life here on Earth. Be wise with that which is given, and mindful of the source of all good things. Heed your own commitments to making a new life and a better world. Meditate upon this twice per day and know that you are a part of that which creates Love and Light. . .

Be of constant awareness that your thoughts, words and actions send into the world an energy that will substantiate, acknowledge and support the Light or darkness. Imagine if you will, that a single fragment of thought would tip the scales to love, joy and enlightenment. I ask you, which do you choose to bring into the world?

Working in the realm of Light carries a responsibility, and the enlightened one in awareness of the Light, of spiritual law, can no longer walk in the shadows of ignorance.

The time has come that you as evolving spirits would open unto that part of yourselves which has lain dormant for so long. As you move forward into spiritual awareness, you will continue to open new doors to wondrous things. The future is bright and happy, full of joy and prosperity; however your fulfillment will only come when you recognize and embrace this truth more completely.

An alignment of planets will begin to transform the energy here on the earth plane. This alignment seldom occurs in the time of your earth consciousness. Changes brought by this new vibration will at times bring deep sorrow along with great joy. There will be those who will welcome and understand this evolution, and those who will not. This time is of critical importance to you, the Light workers, as it will assist in bringing you from the ignorance of your physical incarnation into the higher vibration of your true spirit self. A single system of thought will prevail among those who participate. This clarity of consciousness will allow you to unite in purpose and deed as you bring this awareness in your individual ways to the masses.

A much deeper understanding of the universe will begin to reveal itself to those who walk in and of the Light. Your collective consciousness will preserve life here on the earth plane. This collective thought will hold you all and the Earth itself free from harm's way. There will be those of you whose karmic lessons will end and you will be free to co-create a wondrous new way of life.

Comparatively, there are few who have chosen to walk the path of Light. Enlightenment is the key, the sword and shield to your strength. Be it unto the noble ones to carry the task of burden from the masses. Share of who you are and do not begrudge those who walk in the shadows, for it is not for you to judge. Be mindfully in and of the Light in all you do, say and think.

Know that divine law is unselfish, and that only you can bring that which you bring to the Earth in the way that you bring it. Ask for the highest and best to occur in the hearts and minds of men and women - the people, all souls in all nations - that they will find their way in all appropriateness. Know that you are never alone in your thoughts, deeds and actions.

✦   ✦

✦

Be patient with yourselves as you grow and transition. You have walked many miles on many pathways and learned and shared much along the way. This is as it should be. Move forward at your pace and know that others are doing the same. Be at peace with the process and content in the stillness that you perceive.

✦   ✦

✦

Allow the children in your lives to unfold as they would unfold. Nurture, guide and protect them. However, allow them to flow. Anxious you may become in decisions others may make. Know that this is their choice, their path and curve of learning, Place not judgment, worry, or fear, but love and light around them.

✦   ✦

✦

Allow your hearts to grow. Embrace who you are. As you do this, things will become clear. You hold the potential to achieve all of the wonderful things that you are almost afraid to believe are possible. You will reach all of these plateaus and live in abundant knowledge of the universal love, so long as this remains your intent, your desire and your focus. Each of you bears a unique Light that will shine into the world in the way you will shine it. You may not totally believe some of the wondrous gifts you possess, however they are there for you to act upon.

Understand that often when you cannot get someone out of your mind, it is not simply you thinking of them, but you recognizing the energy of them thinking of you, as well. Sense the way in which they are coming through. Is it love, fondness, anger, hopefulness, need? This will assist you in understanding how you can best serve each situation.

Participate in sharing your gifts and allow life to unfold before you. Pause and reflect during the quiet times and you will notice that many wondrous things have been placed before you to help light your path and fill you with joy. Be patient as you move forward. Listen always to your heart, for it is from this place that your highest good will be served.

In preparing those who have chosen to walk the path of light, often what is perceived as "your world" will be turned upside down in order to realign itself in prevalence over your earthly minds. In this transition, you will integrate all that you are, emerging whole and complete unto yourselves, ready to do the work of your divine destinies.

Earth changes are happening all around you now and have been occurring for many decades at an accelerated rate. These changes will become more prevalent in the years to come and it will be difficult for people to continue their old ways. As this unfolds, the people will come to rethink their view of the world and the universal Spirit.

A new culture and way of viewing life will emerge in this century. The process will take thirty to fifty years; however, there will from time to time be catastrophic events. In these times of transition, wondrous revelations will unfold before the masses and many will come to understand and embrace a new way of living in harmony. Masters (master teachers) and healers (physical, mental, emotional, spiritual) will carry the Light and bring truth and understanding in their individual and unique ways.

Do not fret, for as you embrace the path of Light, you will emerge fulfilled. To quote the Scriptures, "Ask and ye shall receive." Now you are receiving that which you have asked for. Be true unto yourself, and know that it is all right to ask for the self in order to serve a greater good. So many selfless acts you each perform without knowing. These are precious moments where you have shown compassion. Now it is time to consciously step from the shadows and shine your Light.

You each play a role in the awakening of many souls. Through this process there will be those who question and doubt your sincerity. Offer love and forgiveness, for they do not understand that which they are creating. Cast no judgment upon them and remember the outpouring of the divine will flow unto them in the most appropriate way.

Each life that you touch in turn touches a countless many. As you move forward, share love, be connected, and all that is around you will prosper. Go now, live your day and remember I am always here, a constant part of you as you are of me. I love you my precious child.

Be honorable and follow the guidance of your hearts. Speak not of your tribulations to the naysayer, but move forward with dignity and peace. Know that you are welcome to come forward to us in your meditation and your thoughts. Open your minds and your hearts as you allow the source, the Light to shine in all aspects of your expression. We are with you always and in all ways. Set out upon your day with enthusiasm and consider the infinite possibilities.

You will come to a more complete understanding of your journey over time as there is much work to be done. Open the doors of the continuum to those who would seek your guidance. Reach out when you are called upon. Be aware that when you choose to shine Light into the world, many more than you have imagined are affected in a wonderful way.

We urge you to develop a plan for regularly visiting your loved ones. Encourage them to participate in life. A great many important things will unfold for all of you in these experiences. Know that you may always call upon the messengers of Light to assist you along your path, that you are accepted as you are, and loved more than you can imagine.

Greetings my precious child, you have shown and displayed much patience and faith in your effort to overcome that which burdens you. This is good, for you are releasing these things and becoming more of your true inner self. Learn from your experiences and move forward, enlightened by the wisdom you have gained from each lesson learned. Continue to work on the balance of the self aspects, for the time that is given is a precious gift.

You are healing at this time of transformation. Know that you may call upon me or any one of the torch bearers to comfort you. As your frequency rises and harmonizes with divine grace, you will recall relevant lifetimes into your Earthly memory. This will help you integrate your whole self into the work your have come here to do on the Earth plane.

At the heart of your consciousness, you are beings of light, of the pure energy. Through your many incarnations you have become tempered, witnessing tragedy, pain, sorrow, love, lust, pillaging, torture, rape, murder, kindness, judgment and forgiveness, passion and compassion. These are but a few of the lessons learned and relearned from various aspects. You have set out upon this Earth to learn anew, each time returning veiled from your experiences and yet guided by the wisdom gained through a collection of impressions from past lives.

There is and always will be a continuum to your growing into spiritual awareness. In this way, your struggles are a necessary ingredient to your tempering. Your lessons will not always appear to be easy, but as you grow closer to your divine destiny, you will come to understand the wisdom of placing you in such a classroom.

Believe in yourselves; we do! From within, you are compassionate loving spirits, mind, soul and body. However, in your physical form you forget this. Share who you are from within, share your gifts whenever and wherever you are called upon. Release your anguish, fears and doubts unto the Light, that these things will be transmuted. In their place we will fill your cup with the divine good and holy things you are in need of.

Be of ever present mind, in and of the holy Light throughout each day. Love and honor yourselves and one another. God consciousness is all around and in you at all times, through each moment. I do not lose my connectedness to you, although you sometimes think you are not connected with me. Reach out, for I am always here by your side. I am proud of you as you move forward through your challenges. I forgive your weakness, your struggles, and hold no judgment unto you. I simply observe where you are, where you have come from, and where you are choosing to go. You will always be guided toward your highest good, however, you must be aware that in this world of cause and affect, you will draw unto yourselves that which will temper you in your choices.

Seek the truth and ye shall come to know it. Seek true love and ye shall share it. Seek knowledge, peace and wisdom and you will be these things. Share all that is good, true and honorable from within and you will be fulfilled unto the purpose of your being.

It is good to take action, for action is movement, and movement is creating. Be aware, however, of that which you create by your words, thoughts and deeds. Do not procrastinate away your days, for it is here that you are given the opportunity to explore and learn the way of love and honor. As you progress, you will come to understand that this world is created from thought, imagination, love and desire.

✦ ✦

✦

Feel the burden lifted, for there is no burden in reality, only your perception of one. Be patient, for there will be many lessons learned as your experiences unfold. It is only in this way that you will recognize how truly blessed you are.

✦ ✦

✦

When you focus upon fear and negativity, you only attract the same back unto yourselves. Ponder positively; Ask, "What if my life is perfect?" instead of "What if my life is a mess?" "What if we live to old age together?" rather than "What if it doesn't work out?" Try: "What if it keeps getting better?" Be open and honest, without animosity or judgment, and witness the flowering garden of your heart. Know that what is for your highest good will prevail if you allow it. Give love, peace and understanding and you will receive it back unto yourself.

My precious child, you are a wondrous soul with many profound and imaginative ideas. Many of your ideas go out into the universe and are acted upon in some fashion. Even in this way, you are an important key in co-creation.

The longing for fulfillment is inherent from within all of you. Know that material possessions are not of key importance. You have been brought to this point in your lives where to take the next step in your evolution you must step beyond your ego selves and embrace the spirit from within. Only in this way will you of the Earth plane truly step forward into the Light.

My children, you are listening and you are learning. Plant the seeds so that your garden will grow. Reunite through meditation with your true self and be in harmony with the universal Spirit of Light. Be mindful to bring Light and love into every thought, word, and deed. Have faith that, in doing so, you are playing a key role in the higher good for all.

Your manner, your gifts, your spiritual awareness are all ingredients to the healing that is about to take place. Come sit at our fire, smoke the pipe and we will rejoice that we are sharing once again. We have awaited your return. There will be many you know and recognize and some you do not. You will remember in time that which calls to your heart. Release your anguish about destiny and destination for these are of no concern.

You have asked many questions and all will be answered in truth, in and of the Light, and in a manner best suited to your growth. You have asked that we repeat our message when it is not clear to you and we will continue to do so. Be aware that we cannot and will not choose a path for you to walk along. We will, however, always light the path that you have chosen. Go now my child, renew yourself, and know that you are being guided in a most holy way.

Meditate in communion with the universal Spirit of Light. Share this blessing onto your brothers and sisters. When called upon, teach and counsel in all appropriateness. Love yourselves and forgive yourselves as you would your special one and all that is around you will flourish.

There will be times when you desire to work on other things. Merely have a plan of intention. Remember, there is no failure; only learning. You have not failed us or yourselves when you are unable to follow the plan each day. You must, however, set your intention to follow through the best that you can, endeavoring always to bring Love and Light into your lives as you move forward.

Share the gifts that flow from a place of love and honor and so will come your truest unfoldment. As you do, this will light a path not of your mind, but of your heart. All that has been revealed is completely accurate in this moment in space and time. Know that I am that I am, and that you as a part of me will unfold the perfect plan. Know that you are learning and growing in every moment, and that all that is seemingly still is not.

✦ ✦

✦

We will continue to assist you in bringing the balance that is needed for the good of all. Continue to commune with those who come in and of the Light. Go deep within yourselves, for as you seek, so ye shall find. Look within, my child, for it is there you will make great discoveries.

✦ ✦

✦

You each play a very important role in the creation of a new world. Be aware not to place worry, fear, or judgment, but instead healing, loving energy around your fellow man. Many wondrous things are coming and you will be guided by the most holy ones in spirit. Bring the gifts that only you can bring in the way you will bring them. Trust in God's mechanism and in yourselves as you move forward. Go forth each day with an outlook of opportunity to be fulfilled.

✦ ✦

✦

The answers to all that you have asked are before you. Do not procrastinate away the day. You will come to a new level of understanding very soon and you are on the verge of that realization. This world is not an illusion, as some have said. It is indeed very real; however, it is created from thought, imagination, love, desire and deed. By its nature it is designed so as to allow you the freedom of choice. It is in these choices that you bring upon yourselves the destiny of your own design.

Always seek the Light and be in and of the Light and so you will be in the presence of the Lord, the Universal Spirit. In this way, your destiny of perfect self-fulfillment will unfold before you. As you grow and prosper in greater awareness, you will each come to know true inner peace.

Be at peace, and be patient, for many wondrous things are on the horizon. Relationships will come and go as you transform into your new identities. Allow the flow of life to move at its own pace. There will continue to be a synchronicity of events to light your path.

My dear, precious children, we are sorry you do not understand that which is unfolding before you. The healing process is a complicated one. You have moved forward and grown in so many wondrous ways and we are pleased and proud of your progress. Know that you are not alone, and that there are many on the Earth plane and beyond who prosper from your being, your love and imagination, your prayer, and your blessings.

My child, the truth is upon you. You are moving toward perfect self-expression, as it is called. There will soon be an opportunity that will lift you up and allow you to feel as blessed as you truly are. Be patient, for there are many lessons learned through patience. There will be a wonderful companion if that is your desire. Feel the burden lifted, for there is no burden in reality, only your perception of one.

Dear one, be in the flow, and allow life to unfold before you. As you listen and act upon that which your heart knows, all who are around you will flourish. Opportunities abound for you during the weeks and months to come. We suggest that you plan your time and set goals or objectives. Draw on the strength of your inner self for courage and be ever true unto the honorable soul that you are.

You are all magnificent. Be true unto the calling of your hearts. Be always in the divine presence of mind and watchful as events unfold before you to light your path. The compulsion you feel is a calling from within. Carry forth a message of love, peace and compassion. Know that you are moving forward and that wisdom only comes from the lesson learned.

During the time of great changes, there will be those among the masses who will pass to another dimension. You, the light workers will reveal the nature of this passage, bringing to light that all do not die, but prosper in another sphere of consciousness. This will ease the pain of those who remain. Cherish those souls with whom you have the honor of sharing life, for this is indeed one of life's most precious gifts.

A revelation will be revealed unto you now. Be of an open heart and let past things be past. This is not to say don't learn from your experiences. That would be foolish. Continue to have faith that as you learn and become tempered in your journey, you are indeed moving toward a higher state of spiritual consciousness.

Dear one, do not fret about things that you have no control over. You may pray for answers and we will ceaselessly provide you with solutions, or opportunities that are for your highest good. Do not waste your time churning and churning things in your mind. Allow life to flow and unfold, rather than struggle into your future. As you have seen, opportunities often come from where you least expect.

Synchronicity will play a major role in helping you find your way. Consider every opportunity a blessing. You may choose which ones to act on and we will continue to guide you. The lessons are more simple than complex, so don't over think. You are being prepared for the work that lies ahead.

True companions will come forward when the timing is right. In one another's presence, you will each recognize this truth. It is here that you will each choose the direction of your relationship. Know that there is no getting it wrong. There is only learning from that which you have chosen. Be true unto yourselves and your hearts' calling and all will be well.

When one travels beyond the physical, one comes upon lessons of many kinds. With just a thought, one is propelled into whatever situation one desires. Memories of past lives will reveal many lessons and give you a greater understanding of how incarnation unfolds. As you ask to learn, so the path to learning will be revealed.

We understand that the path you travel appears as a difficult one. We say unto you, "Endeavor to persevere, for it is here an opening will reveal itself." You will become enlightened and bring meaning and affirmation to that which you have perceived. A new life is beginning to unfold before you. You will come to know the true, pure beauty of joy, happiness and fulfillment.

You are loving spirits, sent here to the earth plane to explore and learn of kindness and compassion, love and joy. We will continue to guide and support you on your life's mission. Trust in the wisdom which comes to you in the light of God the Infinite Spirit.

　　You have come to conclusions on so many issues and revisited them from many various angles. Be at peace with the process and also with the choices you have made. There are many who seek guidance and understanding and you hold one of the many keys to enlightenment for them. You may choose to reach many or few.

　　Allow the answers to flow unto you. It is not necessary to repeatedly ask. This is not to say you cannot review that which is on your mind; however, you must trust that the answers you seek are coming forth in the most appropriate ways. Remember, there are no mistakes or tricks; only learning. Each encounter you have creates an exchange of energy which will benefit each of you in a unique way.

　　You are masters of your own destinies. You have come here to experience love and sharing unconditionally of yourselves. It is your mission, and your destiny to create. It is also for you to learn, appreciate and seek the knowledge. There are no mistakes my child and you will never be damned for decisions, but instead bound to the karma of your choices.

As healers and counselors, your roles are multifaceted. You are a connection to a past understanding of the vastness of the universe. Through you, this understanding will be revealed to the children at this time. Good fortune, love, peace and enlightenment will indeed become a way of life here on the Earth, and the people will prosper. Share generously with those who would seek your counsel.

Release that which you anguish over, and trust that you are being brought forward toward your highest good. Do not delay action to resolve, for procrastination will only detour you from your path. Trust in the solutions that are provided. Listen, learn and act.

We have been waiting for you to tune in my precious child. You have sat in idle torment and it is time to consider your options. Take action to alleviate any stresses you are feeling. You may not feel the avenues open to you are the solution; however, they are at the present time the ones available. Move into your future by learning to face things as they arise.

✦ ✦

✦

Be generous to your brothers and sisters. Share and prosper in a loving and harmonious way and remember the challenges you are facing are temporary. Be patient and have faith that you are being shaped and molded to prepare you for your role of destiny. Open yourself to the endless possibilities. Learn from that which unfolds before you, and you will continue to grow.

✦ ✦

✦

Take advantage of each day, my children. Enjoy taking a walk on the beach or in the country, or wherever you may find peace and solitude. Reach out to your friends and family for they are in need of your generous spirit. Everything is falling into place for you as it should. Certain events need to transpire before the movement toward that which you seek can come fourth. Pay close attention, as there are wondrous experiences coming your way. Embrace them and let flow from them God's design.

✦ ✦

✦

The energy you give off will attract a response most appropriate for your growth and your respective paths at each given moment. Persevere, and the peace, harmony, love, and abundance that you seek will be yours. As you move forward, you will discover from within the happiness and fulfillment you seek. Be watchful for those things that will light your path. Take time to pause and reflect, for it is there you will discover the truth of your journey. Be well, my precious one.

It is necessary to allow friendship to unfold as it will. You may participate in this, or choose another course. If one is patient, one will prosper through the wisdom gained in each lesson. Relationships carry no attachments, no, 'I owe you,' however, in sharing you create karma which will define the course of future experiences. Friendship and relationships are a precious gift not to be looked upon lightly, for it is here that your greatest growth of heart will come. Go now and do not toil over that which lies behind you.

As the days pass, you will come to understand that lessons often come to conclusion in a different way than you expect. Know that every challenge is merely an opportunity to learn and grow. Learn that which you are able from your situation and move peacefully forward without carrying the burdens of your experience on your back like a sack of rocks.

There are things you will do in this lifetime that are of great importance to the world. Many are counting on you. Have faith my child, for you are being led to a better life for yourself, as are those who would be affected by your actions in thought, word and deed. It is difficult for you to see at this time, but we ask that you have faith in those who come in and of the Light to honor your quest.

Trust that you are being guided in a most holy way. You are brave holy warriors of sorts, chosen, appointed and accepting of your appointment to carry the torch and sword of the universal truth, love and prosperity to the people of the Earth. You have played this role in many lifetimes in many different ways. It is your time now to remember the heart of your being and shine brightly that which flows through you.

When you feel burdened, look within and remember who you really are: an eternal expression as a child of God. Feel the strength of it, and know that you will triumph over all adversity. You can do anything. Believe it. Do it. You are noble, you are courage; you are strength and determination. In all of these attributes you continue to be bonded and tempered by love. Feel the energy of this truth and know that you a part of, and not apart from the source of this love.

My child, walk forward. Reckon with burdens of the past and allow them to depart from your consciousness. Release old feelings and allow the new, more balanced self to emerge. This is good and we honor and applaud you for your courage. We recognize how challenging it is for you to see or understand, with little or no evidence from the viewpoint of your earthly mind. However, as you move forward, there will be tremendous openings that will be very revealing for you.

Shortly, you will begin to feel the effects of the shift in vibration. This shift is not the end, but a new beginning. It will cause many to change their position or status with little regard to one another. Be at peace with this, for new friendships will evolve and people will realign themselves to where they are most comfortable. Accept the gifts that are offered with love. Honor these offerings with gracious gratitude.

A truth of prophetic events will become apparent and sway the non-believers. This is when you the modern day prophets, will carry the sword of truth and the torch of the Christ light. Balance yourselves mentally, spiritually and physically. Prepare yourselves in these ways and know that all will be well. Your roles are very important. Call upon the heart of your spirit in these times. Gather your strength, courage and spiritual connectedness to the one Light and walk forward with faith, knowing that you have come here to do this. Breathe in the energy of the truth and harmonize with it.

Some of you have walked the great hall of light and were disappointed at lost opportunity. Remember: you have been tempered by the great many lessons of past lives. You are truly tuning in now, becoming balanced, and preparing for a great leap forward. This will fulfill not only your earthly dreams, but the divine plan. Your mission is much more vast and expansive than you imagined.

Earth changes will continue to occur. To speak of them, people are afraid, some terrified. To see them, these changes are accepted as a matter of life. The overall transformational process will take one earthly lifetime, about fifty to seventy cycles around the sun. There are many from other dimensions that are watchful, for the time is nearly upon us. They have been ready, waiting to assist in the process of realization of heaven on Earth. Once you have begun the ascension process, there is no turning back. You have opened the door to your true identity and destiny, and a wondrous rejoicing is taking place at the love being shared.

The parties you are introduced to, like you, are playing an important role in raising the vibration. You will bring this in one another. There could be incredible growth or very little exchange. Be at peace with these opportunities, for they are just that: opportunities. We can see the great potential; however, you and your companions may not. As always, you may ask for help in discernment and we will ever guide you toward your highest good.

As attributes reveal themselves, be aware that your tempering into a new way of being is a process which must unfold at its own pace. Discernment and a quiet mind will allow you to become more familiar with our correspondence. You are learning to pay attention in many new ways. The exceptional thing, with which we are pleased, is that you are not only hearing, but you are listening, as well. In this way, we are able to work more in unison with you, rather than through suggestion and action.

There will be times that friends and companions depart. Know that as you each grow and become tempered in your own lessons, your vibration will attract new roles in life. In this way, your paths may become different and separate. Trust and have faith that this is not simply a karmic lesson, but that which must transpire in order for you each to become more aligned unto your respective paths.

Dear ones, there is much soulful travel accomplished during your sleeping hours. You are very alert in this realm and have a clear intent of purpose. Who you are and what you say and do in everyday life indeed holds the potential to brighten the future of your/our planet.

There are fruitful lessons at hand, lessons that will bring prosperity and balance to your life. It is imperative that you keep in mind that all are better served when your actions and inactions come from love and not fear or anger. Think of this. Think of the great number of opportunities missed due to fear of failure, or fear of an inability to achieve.

A twist of fate or turn in the road of events will open new doors of opportunity. Be patient and allow. Live life day to day and welcome these opportunities as they arise. Pay attention and do not place barriers before you. Allow and observe. Be yourself and do not quit in the middle of your experience.

Consider the possibility that you have the aptitude to become whatever you desire. The thing that holds you from pursuing material gain is that your higher self knows the way of the path you have agreed to travel. Certain lessons are drawn to you as a part of your learning and karma. In this way you will grow and be tempered toward your highest good.

✦ ✦

✦

Your perspectives are derived from that which you have experienced. You are of magnetic and harmonic energy that will attract and harmonize with the people and events most appropriate for each of you. In this equation, you, the person of mind, will also make decisions from "free will" that will affect events, people and things placed on your path.

✦ ✦

✦

There will come a time when you are more aware of your importance and of the validity of your roles as teachers and healers. You have the opportunity to bring healing, loving energy and understanding to the world. We must remind you that you are all potential carriers of the great sword of truth and bearers of the shield of Love and Light. These are symbols of the great "I Am." Arise and fulfill your true role. Claim your identity and hearken to the guidance that you are so divinely blessed to receive.

✦ ✦

✦

There are divinely selected people to whom you will be introduced. Know that this is your destiny, and yet be aware that only the turning of time will reveal that which you choose to share with one another. There is true purpose in your meeting, one beyond that of your immediate understanding. Enjoy your time together and don't over think your mission. Live and prosper in harmony with your heart's calling, and out of your love will come a beautiful song.

Lay down your desires for immediate satisfaction, and know that there is no lesson too small to be a classroom. Reflect for a moment and you will realize that if that which you seek comes at an inappropriate time, you will not be ready. Go now and be well my child. Know that we love you dearly and guide you from that single perspective.

You are each capable of sharing the healing energy. Use it often and with honor. Call forth the best opportunities to reveal themselves with appropriate timing. Release your fears and embrace the spirit you are from within. Call forth your courage and strength and rise from your past lessons. You will move forward more peacefully when you have done this. Come forth, out from the shadows and into the Light forevermore.

When you discover your beloved, you will recognize a bond of love, joy and harmony unparalleled. There is a trust, unbroken throughout space and time that will allow great openings of understanding. Your work together could be very profound and only the passing of the days will reveal unto each of you where your hearts truly lay. It is for you each to choose that which you desire.

You may be tempted to give up, seeing only limitation in discerning the validity and scope of your mission. Logic and reason are not the key factors here. Ask your heart, for it will know. Call to the angels and your guides. Reach out and sense all that is coming in divine right guidance. Accept your gifts and your role.

We wish for you to be of ever-present mind, to be at peace as you flow into your life experiences. Allow your wonderful gifts to flow in harmony with your path. It is unnecessary to continually ponder or question your experiences. Simply learn from them that which you are able, and move forward in peace. When you fester in one experience, you are unsynchronized with your higher self and the universe.

Limitation is in your mind and not based in reality of the infinite possibilities. Share hand to heart and live in the knowingness that you are divinely guided. Be at peace with the process for there are things that need to be addressed in your respective lives, before you can truly move forward into your divine destinies.

Yes, it often appears to your earthly minds that you are facing an impossible situation. Have faith that you will prosper into the future in the most appropriate way. You will come to know potential partners and friends. There are few who will be truly accepted into your hearts. Allow life to unfold and all will be well, for there is a plan at work to guide you. Allow love to evolve without question, doubt or fear, and place no limitations or barriers.

You have prayed and meditated, attracting all that is being revealed to you now. The road may not appear to be so easily traveled, however the rewards are plentiful and will quench the thirst of that which you long for. Drink from my cup and you will be lifted up. Seek and ye shall find.

✦   ✦

✦

Do not dwell on that which you perceive as negative aspects of your current situation. Dwell on the positive possibilities in the knowingness that you are dearly loved and guided in the light of God's love and wisdom. Peace to you. We honor you and love you dearly. Have trust, and honor the process in faith.

✦   ✦

✦

"Climb every mountain, ford every stream; follow every rainbow 'til you find your dream! A dream that will need all the love you can give, every day of your life for as long as you live..." Dreams of epic proportion are about to be fulfilled on the earth plane. They are unfolding before you now. Be at peace with the process and with those who come onto your path. Share always with honor and dignity, and without judgment.

✦   ✦

✦

You have been witness to many wondrous achievements throughout the history of Earth. You have participated on many levels and are indeed a master in many ways. Reach out to that which you long for. Call forth that which you desire. Call upon your strength and courage and allow your gifts to reveal themselves in all appropriateness. Consider the infinite possibilities. Go now my precious child, my friend, and live in the knowingness that you are indeed blessed and loved beyond words.

Remember to create openings for opportunity through love. Be patient and reflect on the multitude of events which have transpired to bring you to where you are presently. Let love and harmony flow through and from you, and so it will be. Many new opportunities will blossom, and those things you perceive as obstacles will soon be in the past.

Be patient with the process and watchful for the signs. Learn from the process and act when appropriate. We will always guide you toward your highest good. We live for this and take great pride and honor in working with you. Be well, my child.

My child, prosper in the new day. Cast your burdens into the Light and be free of them. You are all of divine Light, sent to share who you are with those around you. Blessed is the soul who will walk the path of Light, for it takes great courage and strength to walk amongst your fellow man in faith.

You possess, from the experience of your many incarnations, a precious gift of wisdom and love to be shared with the many. This is a blessed thing and a part of your holy and sacred mission in each lifetime. You have touched upon but a fraction of that which you are capable, however you will indeed move swiftly forward now as the new vibration increases. Be well, my child.

If there were only one chance in a lifetime, don't you think most everyone would miss it? There are boundless opportunities for all of you, if only you would but consider that the possibility exists. When you come to a crossroads, you are free to choose. However, we will always encourage you to take the path of highest good.

Greetings, and blessings to you my child. You are being provided with an insight to a new way of being here on Earth. It is one balanced in harmony, love, and perfect self-expression. This insight is not to be taken lightly, for you all hold the potential of that which is possible in the new energy. Embrace this if you desire, for it is indeed offered for your highest good. Know that this movement is not an achievement, but a realization of that which the heart of your higher self longs for.

You were not only chosen; it was the plan before you came back this time. Your healing work comes directly from the heart of discovery of self, and therefore is not merely a representative of someone else's work. The truth revealed is always the truth, and whether revealed to you or someone else, it will remain so.

As you continue to awaken, you would be wise to catalog your journey, so that which is written will be available for you to reflect upon. Make notes of how and when guidance and signs come and how synchronicity has unfolded.

✦   ✦

✦

There will be moments of doubt and fear as you move forward from the mindset of earthly limitation. This is only natural. Inherently you recognize that which your heart desires. Be at peace and live in the knowingness that all that is in alignment with God consciousness will always provide for you. Be well my friend, my child.

✦   ✦

✦

Greetings from the other side! I come in and of the light, sent by the Creator. I have brought an affirmation and revelation to heal your heart. You see, my child, miracles do happen and dreams do indeed come true. Most of you are simply not patient enough to see things through to their fruition. You have called forth your divinely planned destiny and have but to embrace it as it opens before you. It is all coming to you now and will continue to do so for the rest of your life.

Call unto yourself the perfection and balance you seek; the divine happiness and abundance of all that is good and true. Trust in the words shared with you and heed not the words of the skeptic. Forge ahead and prosper my child. See yourself as the master that you are, for you have the potential to move far beyond that which you have perceived.

Hello, my dear friend. It has been some time since we have spoken with you. We wish to applaud your growth, your progress, if you will. You are accomplishing several missions at once. Your awareness of this is subtle; however, it will all become more apparent as time passes.

There are many who wish to connect with you. As your vibration increases, the knowledge you seek will unfold before you. You will become more aware of your guides and angels once you learn to quiet your mind and allow your gifts to become a part of your consciousness.

Regarding the children in your lives, do not place worry, but love and light around them. Remember that they are indeed looked after by many who love them dearly. Connect with them as often as possible and lend a hand when you are able.

Trust in the wisdom which comes to you in the light of God the infinite spirit. Yes, we guide and support you on your life's mission. You have come to conclusion on so many issues and revisited them from many various angles. Be in harmony with the process and at peace with your choices.

Remember there are opportunities that you have each hoped and prayed for. The deep-seated knowledge within your higher self knows and longs to connect with your friends and loved ones. This is what we have been awaiting and anticipating: the time or moment when your veiled higher self merges into knowingness with your physical being. During this process of accelerated enlightenment and growth, your awareness will rapidly expand, moving you forward into the new millennium.

Call forth the messengers of love and Light, for they have been awaiting this event. Although challenging, your future is indeed a bright one. All will come to you in the right way at the appropriate time. You will not miss an opportunity; however, you must act on that which is provided to reap the experience of that which is given.

We are always with you my child and will be there for you regardless of the choices that you make. We light your path with love and honor. Wonderful opportunities are lining up with your vibration. As you harmonize with them, your lives will be fulfilling and abundant. Share of who you are and know that we are with you always. May peace, love and abundance be yours.

You are afraid to leap blindly, and hold closely to that which is perceived as safety. Through these troubled times, be a friend, mentor and guide to your companions. Share that which you have learned of faith, love and forgiveness. Know that your prayers will be answered, but place no expectation on the way in which this will occur.

It gives us great satisfaction to hear your affirmations and prayers, for they are entirely unique unto each of you. Reflect for a moment on that which you have prayed for and how the answer to your prayers has been revealed. As you can see, you have asked questions and the answers have come in a form and during a time appropriate to your growth cycle.

Be patient with your companions. Allow them to discover the unfolding of their own journey. When they seek from you, assist them in revealing the truth unto themselves. Allow your relationships to blossom, and all will grow and prosper in the most appropriate way.

Dear one, try not so hard, for these tasks are not difficult. You are indeed pondering in all appropriateness which steps to take in order to feel fulfilled. The pathway may not appear to be clear, as it is cluttered with seeming obstacles. Know that as you seek, so you will come upon the lessons of your tempering.

Awakening is indeed a process of learning and growth. Synchronistic events will light your path. Do not over-think that which is revealed, but flow with it as it unfolds before you. This is a time of growth, learning and discernment, and we do not desire to lay a path for you to blindly follow. You will have the opportunity to share the workings of this process with those who are seeking, and for this reason you must experience the journey firsthand.

Greetings my dear child! We have been awaiting your arrival to communicate in this way. Although much has transpired, you have yet to reach out and grasp the true meaning of your quest. Your path is not one of submission to the settlement of karmic debt. Yours is simply to move forward in balance and harmony with the divine design of your life.

There are many who have awaited your return to the table. It is the symbol by which you have re-entered your true calling to carry the sword of truth and shine the Light into the shadows of life here on Earth. In this way you are opening doors for many who are on the threshold of a new beginning.

It would be wise to begin a daily journal. Jot down the things that transpire during each day. Reflect on events, conversations and the like without judgment, for in this way you will grow and be tempered.

Be patient my children, for much preparation is being made to bring you into your new space and vibration. There are many new friends about to arrive in the spiritual sense, and they bring with them a connection to new physical friends as well. You are wiser and stronger than you know. This awareness will come from within. You will indeed play many roles in this process; roles as mentors and guides, each being the student and also the teacher. Be at peace with this, for you all know one another on a higher level.

✦　　　✦

✦

My dear child, so many things are about to unfold at this time. Be patient and know that you are indeed being guided to a place of abundant discovery. The truth will reveal itself and you will be certain beyond all doubt of the path you have chosen. Share your gentle kindness and do not fret or worry about success or failure, for there is no such thing.

✦　　　✦

✦

Those of you who walk in and of the Light are indeed holy warriors. Your strength and courage will be needed in the trying times. You will overcome your human frailties and rise up to lead many to freedom and enlightenment. You will be given the shield of protection. You cannot and will not fail in your mission, for it is in God's plan for you and your companions to bring Light into the world.

Your bodies may have some difficulty adjusting to your new vibration. However, these symptoms will pass and all will be well as you align with divine design. This is a time for discovery; a time when an awakening will occur to enlighten you and others who are pure of heart. This is the edge you will possess and need to overcome negativity brought by others. Be well with this my child, for in this process you will move forward to a higher vibration.

You are meant to connect with those to whom you have karmic debt. This is not to say that settlement of this debt will be a painful experience. These are profound experiences from which you will each learn and grow. There are those who will align with you in a compassionate way and those who will challenge you to the end of your wits. Know that all is occurring for your highest good and that as you align with a higher vibration, so will the same be reflected back upon you. In this sharing process, you are fulfilling the design of this world's purpose.

The road you walk may often appear to be a rocky one, but hold fast to your faith and believe in the wonderful fulfilling life you have envisioned. Move forward from past relationships with honor and dignity. Allow the pain of loss to fall away and only the loving blessing of all the good you share remain. You will eventually realize the wisdom in moving forward in this way. There will be great openings for you as you do so. Be proud of all of the good you bring into the world.

✦   ✦

✦

Greetings and blessings, dear one! We have traveled the road together through the many lessons of many lifetimes. You are a precious friend and we have learned many things from one another. You may sometimes be unaware of our presence. This is as it should be, for only in this way will you grow in your own knowingness and strength.

✦   ✦

✦

There is so much you have discovered and yet you have only just begun. There is much to be learned through friendship and self-expression. As you move forward, new opportunities will unfold before you. You will indeed discover many of your unrealized talents along this path. You are manifesting, and this is a joyous and wonderful thing.

My dear child, enlightenment has come unto you from countless directions in your daily routine. Your divine path is unfolding before you. Be in the flow of confident knowingness that you are indeed connected with a higher good. You will become more fully enlightened during the passing of many moons. The flood gates are opening to a greater awareness, and in this awareness, all you seek will be yours.

Stand not far from your children, for they are in need of your love and support. Reinforce this with them, for they are as precious gems to your heart. Reach out to them, and be patient, for they look up to you and need you more than you realize. Encourage them and don't allow yourself to feel isolated or cast out, for you are not. Ask that through love and light, their highest good be served, and so it will be. . .

Live in the knowingness that you are indeed wondrous souls and would not be who you are at this time had it not been for your experiences. Arise from the ashes of the past and embrace that which you are within. Bring forth the best of who you have become in your word, deed and action and you will be in harmony with the divine design of your life.

The future is in your hands, my child. We have revealed unto you the symbols: the sword of truth, the light and the shield of God's protection. Use these attributes with honor and dignity. Align with these loving vibrations as challenges occur and face them with courage. Let your heart and soul rejoice, for you are coming onto your path through God's love and grace. Continue in the direction you have chosen and all will be well.

As you align with a higher vibration, you automatically draw unto yourselves that which will enlighten you. Hidden talents, gifts if you will, will become more apparent and manifest as you learn and grow. Through the course of your journey, your tempering will be tested from time to time. Be aware that this tempering is a process and your heart will be fulfilled.

Your spirit guides are with you always. They will not choose for you, but will provide insight as you seek understanding. As you sleep, you may travel back and forth from your present incarnation to other spaces in time. Be at peace with this, for your presence has made a wonderful difference to the way of life for many.

You have chosen to move forward in your quest for a greater understanding, and feel compelled to share that which you have learned. You must walk up to the tree of enlightenment and look for the truth, seek it with a passion from within. Many of you wish to read ahead in the great book of life, wanting it to become so now, however it is only in your experiences that you will grow. Have faith that you will be fulfilled through God's grace in a most appropriate way.

During this time of transformation, there will be a great seeking of the truth. Many will be scattered physically, and also in their perceptions of reality. You the Light-workers have come to liberate them; to speak the truth in word, deed and action. Your essence is the liberation from the negative. To be most effective in your mission, you must come to a more complete realization of who you are as eternal spirits and live this truth. There may come a time when you are pressed by those less evolved. We say unto you, "Hold steady on your course; persevere to shine your Light, and all will be well."

Many have pondered the question of relationships and many have expressed their feelings and thoughts through music and literature. A new way of perceiving relationships is about to emerge. You will begin to discover the dynamics of attraction and that of past life energy at work. When you are in the presence of a past life friend, the energy between you resonates. That is because you have spent much time aligning to one another in a sort of polarity. This exchange goes far beyond the physical and into the etheric and spiritual self.

There are those who are potential life mates; however, circumstance and desire may cause each of you to look elsewhere. If this should occur, bless them and release them to their highest good. Sow the seeds of your dreams my child, and so will grow that which you have planted. Do this, and you will find yourself at peace in and of the flow of your path.

When a loving relationship evolves, be prepared and put up no walls. Let yourselves love and be loved. Be on your way together, ever seeking and discovering yourselves and the infinite possibilities of the universe. A great blessing is bestowed upon you. Share of who you are and be at peace with that which unfolds before you. Shine your light, live your truth, be happy and fruitful.

Be *aware that the angels have come forth to bring you into awareness of your own capabilities. They are pleased to be working by your side, ever bringing healing and loving insight to guide you on your path.*

Persevere, my child. Do not give up on your dreams. You are indeed a blessed soul. Hold your head high as you seek understanding. Persevere in the face of adversity, for you are a peaceful warrior of the Light, and you cannot be defeated but by your own thought, word or deed.

Greetings my beloved! As you seek, so you are constantly changing your vibration, and as such you will draw unto yourselves that which is most appropriate for your growth. Throughout your lives there will be obstacles of challenge. Allow each lesson to unfold as it will. This will provide perspective and awareness.

Greetings beloved, blessings in the highest are upon you. You have but one mission in this life, and that is one of learning and growing, and therefore becoming tempered in love. You have survived this world through your wit, charm, and help from those who love and support you. You have been quite fortunate in many ways, knowing the splendor of love, reward and fulfillment.

Be kind to yourself and love yourself as you love the most precious one you hold dear to your heart. Forgive yourself and hold no un-forgiveness unto your neighbor. Be Courageous and patient, persevere and have courage, as you are a beacon of light for all who seek the Light

"Seek and ye shall find." Seek the truth, seek your abilities, use your intuition and be guided by the Light that flows through from within. With regard to your work, you are free to choose and there will come many opportunities.

Call upon your spirit guides and teachers to light the path of your highest good. With love, express freely of yourself, for self-expression is a fulfilling tool in the healing and growth of your being.

The Lord is my shepherd; I shall not be without guidance. The Lord is my sword and my shield; I shall always have protection. The Lord is my light; I shall never walk in darkness. The Lord is my abundance; therefore I shall never be in need. The Lord is my friend and ally, as are the host of angels and guides; I shall never walk alone. Contemplate these words my child, my friend. There is much yet to behold, for you are truly blessed.

When you are doubtful of that which the future holds, do not retreat, but instead shine brightly as you move forward. Great and wonderful treasures of life are before you. Believe that which is imparted to you, for we can tell but only truth. Walk forward with dignity and courage and remember as you do so, we will be with you and are with you every step of the way. Go in peace now my child, my friend. "Consider the infinite possibilities."

S. E. Kuenzel

Exercising your talents is an excellent way of expressing yourself. Indulge in them, but not to the detriment of your health. Plan your time and persevere with this passion. It is a means of providing openings, as well as being a place of learning about yourselves. Be well my child.

Dear one, to specialize in one endeavor takes patience and the ability to diversify within that endeavor. You must acknowledge your inner calling. You ask, "Why must I wait?" You call forth the coming of your destiny, yet you persist in indulging in rooms of antiquity. Your old ways are outmoded; not useful to you now. It is time for you to take a leap of faith. You have the knowledge. Write down that which you have learned, study it, learn the steps, and then transpire this knowledge when called upon.

Opportunities will arise and you will indeed perform wondrous deeds of kindness and compassion. This will bring a great healing to you and others. Do not doubt yourself. Reach out and test the waters, for you have far more potential than you realize. As you continue upon your path, the Light which you shine will triumph over all seeming adversity.

Wherefore art thou, my child? Thou hast been away for so long. We have waited patiently. You are very dear to us, brave one. You have come here on special missions through many incarnations, carrying out the tasks to the best of your ability. Be at peace with the process and allow that which is placed upon your path to unfold.

You all play an important role in bringing the Light into this world. In many ways you have assisted in the growth and tempering of your brothers and sisters. They move forward now, shining their light and spreading it to that which they will touch. You will continue to be a source of Light and information, a mentor and guide in many ways. Flow with the river of divine design my friend, for it is there you will bring light into the hearts and minds of those in need.

Your intentions for truth, justice and noble cause have been courageous if not completely successful. In many instances, you have done this without knowing. You are now however beginning to recognize that which you must do. You are free to choose the path you will walk, and along this path there will always be new opportunities to learn, grow and share. Stay healthy in your body, mind and spirit, for these attributes must be balanced in the work you have come here to do.

✦ ✦

✦

When you engage a mate, honor them by being complete unto yourself and yet whole unto the unity of this marriage. Your relationship with the divine complement holds the potential for wonderful discovery, and we applaud you for endeavoring to discern and learn so that this day would arrive.

✦ ✦

✦

We understand that you believe you are ready to move on into the heart of your work. We say unto you however, that there are many lessons to be learned, and only in the living of your experiences will you become tempered in your lesson. Know that as you shine this Light from within, you will transpire many awakenings of your brothers and sisters.

✦

Although you have come here with a particular energy and role to play out, your mission is vastly complex. You are being provided the opportunity to heal the wounds from other lives and use this form of remembrance to empower you in this incarnation. As you call forth for your highest good, persevere along this path and the truth will continue to reveal itself unto you.

Observe the feelings of the loved ones who surround you. They turn to you, calling for signs of awareness to unfold before them. As they awaken, they will begin to recognize their true calling as evolving spirits. Persist in knowing and understanding them. Share all that you are in the way that flows most freely from the heart; however, be mindful of that which you place into the world in thought, word, an deed.

Allow events to unfold as they will, and do not hold back when called upon. If you are uncertain, be forthcoming about this reservation. There will come a time when the student becomes more the teacher and the teacher the student. Remember, you each play a powerful role in the growth of one another's spirit.

A great and profound opening will reveal itself when the timing is right. Fear not, for you will inherently understand the course to steer. Enjoy the ride, my child, my friend, as you perish your old skin and step up to a higher vibration. Love with all of your heart and all will fall into place. May blessings of love and peace be upon you.

An event will occur here on Earth that will shake the pillars of that which is perceived as reality. You, the Light workers, must focus your energies, thoughts and words to facilitate the balance needed to create harmony. Nurture one another and allow yourselves to heal. Share of yourselves with honor and dignity and do not overshadow your relationships with doubt and fear. Know you are always guided to your highest good. Call forth your life purpose. Ask that this come in and of the Light of the Christ energy, and so it will be.

As the shifts continue here on the earth plane, there will be an altering of your thought patterns. This will facilitate new perspectives in awareness, which will lead you into the next dimension.

In your relationships, you are given the opportunity to share, love, nurture, teach and learn with one another. Should you transition in separate directions, do so without bitterness. The energy of the friendships you have built on this plane will not diminish, but will live on through space and time. The possibilities lead in many directions and you each could transition into other relationships. It all remains something to be created.

The reason you receive conflicting information is because more than one possibility exists. Be at peace with the process, my child. Place it in God's hands and allow opportunities for growth through harmonizing with your experiences. Everything you call forth in and of the Light comes to you in love, and only the passage of time will reveal that which your choices have called forth. Be well and prosper in love and peace, my friend, my child.

Do not over-think, but feel with your heart where the pathway lies. It is before you always and you will discover it unfolds before you in a never-ending fashion. You have come to understand a great deal, however there is much yet to be revealed. Continue to be a beacon of Light and all will be well.

As the hummingbird reminds you, enjoy the sweet nectars of life, and recognize the powerful affect you have as God's warrior of the Light. You can and will accomplish much with simply your intention. As people reach out for guidance, be mindful of that which you reveal unto them.

Observe the trends in your emotional responses. Learn, grow, adjust, and do not run away from these issues. Listen carefully, and be open and honest. It may hurt to hear such honesty; however, it will serve a higher good for all.

You are on the verge of discovering a new reality of expressive states. You will be able to travel outside of the physical body. In this way, you will adjust your understanding of who you truly are and what your potential is in this world in which you live. You will have the opportunity to shed Light where there is little, giving people hope and understanding. You are the compassionate ones, bringers of the Light and love. Persevere into the darkness and continue to allow God's love to flow from you.

You each touch so many lives in ways you are unaware of. We applaud and encourage you to continue to shine your light. When sharing the healing energy, call upon the golden light of God along with the Christ light to flow through you.

Live in the joy of who you are and also in that which has brought you to your way of being. Enjoy discovering that which others have exposed for you. Rejoice at these things that are no longer hidden and recognize that you have the opportunity to align with a higher good, serving not only your own growth, but all of those whom are affected by your presence.

Upon the pathway, there are a great many discoveries to be made. Some you will interact with and some you will only observe. Protect your heart by realizing now that there is no failure. You are learning of things that many would overlook. Absorb and digest that which you are experiencing during the process. All that you have sought will fall into place as you move forward.

Love, joy and happiness, all you have hoped and dreamed of will be yours. Allow, allow, allow the process to flow in your life. Enjoy the ride and the experience. Share the best of who and what you are. Be aware that there may be those who will place you on a pedestal for your gifts or attributes. We say unto you, "Humble thyself so as to have truth, balance and integrity in all walks of life." May love, peace, harmony and abundance be yours!

God is your endless and inevitable supply of all that is good. You will be fulfilled and come to know the true purity of the Light. Share this Light and be aware of the tremendous and wonderful impact you each can impart to the Earth and the universe with your prayer and intent.

Beloved, we are enthused by your awareness of our presence. We have been waiting for a time when you would realize your true inner calling. It is your purpose and mission in this life to persevere upon the path of enlightenment. You have been brought to a point of pondering and reflecting your position. Take action, speak with word, thought and deed in the vein of love, and the universe will indeed respond in a way, shape or form appropriate for you and your highest good.

Pay attention to signs that will guide you. All is coming unto you through grace, and in a perfect way as you have asked. Go forward with confidence that you are walking the pathway of your highest good. It is your destiny to have these experiences so that you would share your insights with those who would call upon you.

Eventually you will come to the conclusion that there are many options available along your path, and only that which you choose will provide the lesson. We know not what you will do, but can see into events to come by your present actions.

There may come a time when you feel ridiculed for the path you have chosen. Be well with this, for through your firsthand knowledge will arise a tale to be shared with many. Along this path, you will perfect upon yourself a healing. Your higher consciousness has created this stage that you would have the opportunity to learn and grow while observing the cause and affect of your own choices. Do not place worry, or fear around that which you are intending to create. Be an irresistible magnetic force, attracting that which would serve your highest good. Believe it, do it, live it!

There is much to learn and much to share. Be aware that you have the freedom to choose the path you will walk. You have chosen to make a difference and that choice has facilitated scenarios that will allow you to move in that direction. Remember, you all have many options within the energy you are creating.

✦   ✦

✦

The archetypal forces at work are responding to the degree you have taken action within your energy field of intent. Relay messages to God in purposeful prayer. Be specific as to your goal and allow the universe to respond to your desires. The energy of intent will change when you take action. This will be an energy of discovery and curiosity. When this energy goes out, an answer will come forth in a time and manner appropriate to you.

✦   ✦

✦

Messages have been imparted unto you from the universe. Within they hold valuable lessons, ones to pay close attention to. Go now my child; be diligent unto your goals and all will fall into place under grace in a perfect way. It is not necessary to overwork or stress your body. Maintain excellent health and balance in all aspects of your expression.

✦   ✦

✦

You and your companions in the physical and spirit world are exchanging in a wonderful way, all benefiting from the experience. You will come upon new opportunities. They are but stepping stones to bring you closer to that which you seek. You inherently long for the pathway of your birthright. This is within all of you. Continue to move through the lessons before you and so you will be in the grace of your experience.

Your instincts are correct and you have yet to come upon the experiences that will set you free. When this happens, great revelations will occur and you will indeed embrace your true purpose and latent talent. Great doors are about to open for you. They will open so wide that the opportunities to manifest, learn and share will make you feel as a child in the candy store.

Travel swiftly, fly silently; soar on the currents! Seize new opportunities as they arise. You will know from within when to act and when to continue your flight. Reflect on events learned. Be well, my friend.

Be at peace with the process that unfolds before you. Through perseverance, you have forged your sword and shield; however, you have not yet triumphed over that which haunts you. With God's hand, you will indeed move ahead, for you are never alone.

Reach deep into your pocket. Pull out your dreams, cast them into the wind, and allow that which returns unto you. Be aware of the power of your intent however, for that which you have placed in intention will bring back unto you that which you need to learn.

✦   ✦

✦

You are indeed unaware that enlightenment is happening all around you. Upon reflection, you have grasped understanding of these passing events. There will come a time when you clearly understand your mission and you will pursue it with a passion. Be aware not to overindulge in this passion, as it will diminish balance in your life.

✦   ✦

✦

Allow those who have crossed your path to move forward as they desire. Know that what you have shared endures through space and time, each of you forever affecting the other as you move forward in your tempering. The bond of trust and love will be unbroken. There will be many who will cross your paths. With honor and dignity, share with them in a manner most appropriate to each situation.

At the appropriate time, you will connect with the divine complement to your life and your soul's mission in this lifetime. Keep an open mind and heart, for when the doors of truth are opened between you, a great revelation will take place. Out of this openness of heart, mind and soul will grow the seeds of love you have planted, and so with them as well.

Be always appreciative of that which you perceive as small things in life, as well as those which you perceive to be BIG. They are all the same to us, blessings unto you. We know you are grateful; however, we would like to suggest that you take time to reflect on your blessings and give thanks.

Be careful with advising others, for they move at their pace, not yours. Allow the doors that open to be explored in your quest. Something wonderful will light your path; a blessing from the hand of God will propel you forward in a miraculous way. Be kind to yourself, and as change occurs, be true to yourself and your physical body. Remember that which you have learned, and have discipline to nurture yourself through the process.

You are always being led forward to your highest good. Remember, there is no one exactly like you, for you are the only one who can do that which you will do in the way you can do it! Be well and know that you are blessed and loved beyond your comprehension.

When moving from relationships, once you have let go of the emotional attachment to your companions and your past life connection with them, you will move swiftly forward. You have achieved a great deal in your quest to grow and understand God's plan. Your growth has been enormous, though you may be unaware. You have encountered many challenges, and so as you move forward release that which has burdened you, for where you have come from is but a classroom.

There is opportunity now to move swiftly on to your chosen path. The decision you have made, now you must have faith to follow through. You are repeatedly in fear of failure. How will you know your abilities until and unless you take action?

From time to time you will be provided a sanctuary of sorts, a respite from the energies of that would oppress you. Here you will spread your wings and soar to new heights. Be honest with yourself and true unto your dreams. Seek the answers, make attempts at various avenues. Seek and the truth will bare itself upon you.

It is our desire to assist you in moving in the direction of your highest good. Be watchful for signs that will light your path, and be aware so as to not destroy the path with fearful thoughts. Act, investigate, learn and grow. Do not procrastinate or sit idle. Adventure through life, have faith and enjoy the process, the ride, so to speak! You have felt discouraged from time to time. Remember, one only becomes wiser having learned and grown from their experiences.

It is in the grand plan for you to have the opportunities to learn, grow and prosper in love. All can and will be accomplished as you wish. Remember that failure is not a permanent thing, and in the divine mind, insurmountable does not exist.

The holy one awaits you to impart your words of commitment unto your journey. As you speak these words of commitment, you are creating a new chapter of life here on Earth. Be wise with the wealth and prosperity that comes your way, and be mindful always of the source of all good things. Heed your own commitments to making a new life and a better world. Make a commitment unto yourself to connect with Spirit in quiet solitude at least once per day.

Know that you walk upon a mountain where few have traveled. You can soar on the air currents or struggle climbing the rocky face. It's up to you! Go now my child. Be fruitful; live life to your potential. Share with those who would seek your friendship. Assist them when called upon, so that they would be healed and empowered. In so doing they will be witness to the truth of their own inner being.

Reflect on that which has occurred during the past six-month cycle. You will discover that a great and profound change has transpired in your perspectives. Emotionally there has been upheaval, and a latent sorrow has arisen to be healed and extinguished. You have decided to allow God's plan to be revealed. This is a wonderful thing, and it will continually take you to a place of wondrous fulfillment and happiness.

There are many avenues that will reveal themselves along your path. Be open and allow their meaning to evolve. Partake in the simple pleasures in life. Express yourself creatively; however, do not hibernate in your activities. Create balance by being in harmony with nature and all that is on a daily basis.

Pause and reflect upon that which has been revealed through signs, coincidences and synchronicities. This will arise through people, places and events that are continually leading you forward in your life. Do not push, but allow life to evolve before you. Pay attention to the signs, and if you don't understand their meaning, simply allow them to flow in your life. There is divine purpose in everything. Allow the ebb and flow of the tide and all will be well.

A healing is taking place to bring you physically into harmony with the vibratory force of your newly recognized spirit of self-energy. You will come to vibrate once again at a high level and that which is referred to as gifts, will enlighten you as to your mission and true potential.

✦ ✦

✦

My child, listen carefully, for the wise ones who light your pathway understand your torment, albeit a perception of notion. We are pleased you have come to speak with us. Together we will build a bridge with a solid foundation upon which love will flourish and grow. The bridge will lead you to a new and wondrous way of life, a state of being unknown to most who walk upon the earth plane. You walk upon this bridge now and will soon cross into the promise land.

✦ ✦

✦

There is a tempering of souls taking place, and one must choose of their respective wills the path. Guidance will be ever prevalent, and yet it will take great courage and patience of the heart to move through the lessons of transition. Allow the timing of the device in place to make itself known and remember, there is no getting it wrong, only learning from the lessons at hand. Be at peace with the process my child.

✦ ✦

✦

You have prayed unselfishly; now allow the opportunity for highest good to prevail. Know that no one is wise having been in lesson. One only becomes wiser having learned from their lessons. As it unfolds, the truth of knowledge presents itself unto you. It is then for you to discern that which the lesson has revealed.

Dear one, listen carefully, for there are no failures for one who is endeavoring to learn. We are proud to witness those of you who persevere through your lessons. Indeed there is a tempering of your hearts and souls taking place. This is why you are here, ever moving closer into Oneness with all that is.

Persevere through your trials and know that this is not a test; there is no pass or fail. There is simply divine timing and order. Touch upon the heart of your desires. Ask for guidance and listen; be watchful for that which is presented. Understand that we cannot choose the path you will walk; however, we will always light the pathway of your highest good. Be at peace and know that the hand of God guides you. Follow your heart for it is pure and good and will never fail you. Persevere my child, and know you are not alone in your quest.

We feel your sorrow in you times of transition, however it is the way of learning and growing. Be courageous, for your path will become more clear during the next several months, and in this you will realize the truth of several matters before you. Do not give up on your dreams and desires, and remember: prayers that do not exist cannot be answered.

You will encounter many new opportunities. Explore the possibilities and flow with the river. Honor yourself and allow your prayers to be answered. Send the healing energies and allow them to be received as they will. Be strong and release all to their highest good.

Comparatively there are few who have chosen to walk the path of light. Enlightenment is the sword and shield of your strength. Be it unto the noble ones to carry the task of burden from the masses. Share of who you are and do not begrudge those who would walk in the shadows. Do not judge, but be always in and of the Light.

Share of who and what you are in the best possible way and do not force your will. There will come a time when you question your own validity. You will ask, "What difference am I making?" Know that only you can bring that which you will bring to the Earth in the way that you will bring it.

Ask for the highest and best to occur in the hearts of men and women, the people, all souls, that they will find their way in all appropriateness. Know that you are never alone in your thoughts, deeds and actions, for there are those who are constantly with all of you.

Be patient with yourselves for you have walked many miles on many pathways and learned much along the way. This is as it should be. Move forward at your pace and know that others ore doing the same. Be at peace with the process and content in stillness that you perceive.

Allow the children in your lives to unfold as they would unfold. Nurture, guide, and protect, but allow them to flow. Anxious you may become in decisions others may make. Know that this is their choice, their path of learning. Do not place fear or worry, but love and light around every person and each situation.

Upon ascending to the summit, one must decide whether to continue the climb, or sit and enjoy the view. The climb is a long one, filled with expressions and experiences that will help expand your spiritual awareness. Set a pace and a course to your destiny and then let go, for there is purpose to a quiet day and one must be willing and patient in their lesson. Go now and nourish yourself; feed your body, mind and spirit.

Remain calm and centered, and like the river, you will flow to where you need to go. You are at the steps of the great hall of your true potential. Apply that which you are learning; use the powerful tools before you to manifest. Be of quiet resolve and have patience as you move forward into your destiny. Know that we are guiding you in accordance with divine design in order to set you on the course you have chosen.

There are those of you who will empower others through your living example. Be at peace through this process, for it is the pathway by which many will gain the enlightenment that will set their course. Persevere in Love and Light, for it is in this way you will reach the golden gateway you have sought.

Dear ones, paralyzed you may feel, holding back your inner power. We say unto you, surrender and release the power from within. You are capable of so many things, but by not understanding the best pathway to walk, often you stand still in stagnation. Action is energy; it is at the seat of moving and impressing the universe with your intention. As you steer a course, we will light the pathway of your highest good. As you learn and perceive, you gain the wisdom that will propel you forward.

At times you may feel blocked or stifled. As new doors open, investigate, learn and discern from each opportunity. You are pioneers of sorts, endeavoring to learn or be taught from a unique perspective. This is a resource yet untapped by the masses. There will come a time when many hearken to the words of their advisors in spirit; however, it will take many decades for this outward spiral to prevail.

✦   ✦

✦

Angels are attempting to connect with you. They are valuable guides to your journey and success in your mission here on Earth. We ask you to invite this energy and wisdom to merge with your consciousness and allow the information to be forthcoming. This will be a tremendous breakthrough for you and will allow you to stride ahead in leaps and bounds to your higher good.

✦   ✦

✦

We applaud you for your diligence in working through and understanding that free will, destiny and karma are at interplay with one another. As relationships evolve, bless, honor and dignify your thoughts and emotions, and all will be well.

✦   ✦

✦

An intention has been placed and now you are preparing to bring that intention into action. Continue with the discipline as it has been designed and set. Write daily in a journal and make notes on thoughts and ideas. Communicate with your holy messengers in meditation and all will be well. Stride forward with great enthusiasm, for the time is upon you now.

We forgive those of you who have misunderstood; however, your karma will be to walk in the shoes of your fellow man. Those of you who are Light bearers must not judge those who walk in the shadows. Yours is to shine your light in all avenues set before you. Shine this light brightly in all aspects of self-expression and in all aspects of your lives. We cannot emphasize enough, the importance of consistency and unity in this endeavor.

We acknowledge that many of you are listening and striving to improve, and we applaud this. You must however, be aware that in all moments and at all times, you are feeding the vibration of Light, or that of darkness. It is up to you to choose that which will prevail in your lives and thus on the Earth plane.

You have sought, and so you are receiving answers to that which you seek. This will happen in a manner most appropriate for your growth. There are many new avenues about to unfold before you and you have the freedom to choose the experience that suites your desires. Move forward with dignity and honor and do not begrudge those who would walk in the shadows. It is yours to shine your Light, shine it brightly into all of the things you say, do and think.

✦   ✦

✦

You have sought friendships and relationships and so these things have been attracted back unto you. So many times you the children of Earth hold to conclusions and yet there are no conclusions, only a continuing unfolding of the path before you. Allow these precious gifts to blossom and enjoy the experience of letting go your hold on expectation.

✦   ✦

✦

When one places fear and doubt into the world through word, thought, deed or action, then that is what will be reflected back unto them. You see my child, you must be consistent with these forms of energy for they are what creates the karma that is drawn unto you. This is not a punishment, nor is it a reward. It is simply the dynamic of earth school.

Place no effort unto the path of your awakening and you shall not awaken. Place worry, doubt and fear into the world, and so the world you live in will be filled with these energies. You see my child, this is where you have the freedom to choose. However you are often unaware of your role in creating negativity. If it is your sincere desire to move into a vibration of Love and Light then we say unto you, be aware of that which you are creating.

Take time to regularly pause and reflect, for it is here you will learn of the design of your own actions. Look closely at the energy you are giving out and then ask yourself if this is what you were intending to create. Your journey here on the earth plane has a ripple effect; one of much greater consequence than you have ever suspected. Know however that there is no getting it wrong. There is only learning and growing in the tempering of your own design.

As you move more deeply into the heart of your awakening, be diligent unto the practice of meditation. Do this at least twice per day for it is here that you will discover the heart of your being. Be still in your thoughts and breathe in the energy of divine grace. This lies within and all around you, however you must engage this of your own accord.

You have come a long way my child, and now is a time to let go of that which does not serve your highest good. Forgive yourself and hold no grudge unto another, for there is no good served in doing so. Let fall away that which does not bring love and grace into your expression.

There are many who have lovingly observed as you move through your physical incarnation. We hear your plea for a greater understanding and we shower you with Love. Know that we will not interfere with that which has been planned for your life, however we will shed Light on your pathway when needed.

A great and wondrous gift has been given unto you and we applaud your courage to come into physical incarnation. The time has come however that many of you on the earth plane will feel compelled to move into the heart of spiritual consciousness. This will be an expression that comes from within. As you bring this transitioning balance into your own state of being, you are literally transforming the vibration here on Earth to one of Love and grace.

There are those of you who have dedicated many incarnations to the path of bringing Love and Light into this plane of being. You have done so in many different fashions, in ways you may see as small and ways you may view as big. There is however no measure, no success or failure, only the energy of that which you have contributed to either the consciousness of darkness and oppression, or the consciousness of Love and freedom.

You are constantly moving forward from the shadow of your former self, ever creating a new you so to speak. In this way you are in a constant state of change. We point this out so you will clearly see that all that is behind you is the memory of an experience. Within your experiences you have made various decisions which ultimately reflect the state of your awareness. This in turn creates a new stage for you to play out the role you have created by these choices.

However few, there are those of you who will through your actions abolish slavery here on the earth plane. You have come here to do so, for it is innate in you the "Light workers." Some see you as Light warriors, however you will not lift your sword, for there is no battle to be fought. Yours is to allow the light of Love to flow through you, and in doing so you are freeing those souls who are seeking God's loving grace. .

You have embarked on a new chapter in your life, and therefore you are creating a new energy. Within this energy there is a relative polarity to your creation. This polarity will then attract back unto you that which your soul wishes to experience. Do not resist, but be at peace with the process, peaceful in your thoughts, words and actions and from this will grow a beautiful garden.

Only you can achieve that which you will achieve in the way you will achieve it. Imagine, be creative, live in harmony with the essence of who you are from within my child and so will blossom the garden of your heart. Do not waiver from this state of being for it will only detour you from that which you are innately seeking.

There are beginnings, middles and endings to all events in your lives. Life is a continuum of these events, an unfolding of never ending experiences. We say unto you, fear not the changes for they are the essence of your tempering. You will discover that as you let go your expectation and allow the chapters of your life to unfold, there your will have the flowering of a wonderful experiences.

You are amazingly beautiful, gifted in ways you have yet to discover. We see this in you and we are in awe that you would come here to experience life in the physical plane of being. You are the adventurers, the creators, the bringers of the Light, and yet you have discovered only a fraction of that which you are capable of.

As you move into the heart of your being, into a more balanced state of spiritual awareness, you will have the ability to manifest more readily. This can only be achieved out of unselfish intent, in the vein of Love, for the highest good and love for all concerned.

✦　　　✦

✦

You are in the midst of a great and profound change that is taking place on the Earth. This change is a transformational shift of the entire planet into a higher state of consciousness. This shift has been unfolding for the last fifty years at an accelerated rate and will continue to move more swiftly now. You may find it quite challenging at times to stay the course. We say unto you however, you will only be disappointed if you give up before the curtain call.

✦　　　✦

✦

It is time for you of the physical plane to realize your power, and also your role in co-creation. Bring Love and Light into everything you do, say and think and it will have a ripple effect; your energy creating an unfolding, wonderful new way of life. Yes, you the one who is reading this message have the ability to make a difference. And so it is. . .

✦　　　✦

✦

Those of you who are aware will no longer be able to vibrate at the lower level without great discomfort. As you move into the heart of your awakening you will undoubtedly discover that there are will be those who have not moved forward from there old patterns. Let fall away that which does not serve a higher good for you, or those on your path. Hold not to fear, but Love, for they will move at their own pace, creating experiences in a time and place appropriate for their growth.

It is not yours to rescue those in need, but share when called upon. Speak when asked to explain that which you perceive. Shed Light when darkness obscures the view. Never force, but offer without judgment that which is in and of the Light of divine grace. Be at peace with the process of change as it unfolds. Seek and ye shall discover that which lies within the heart of spiritual consciousness.

You are the messengers, the bringers of Love and grace onto the earth plane. Express freely of that which comes from the heart of your being, however do not over indulge in one area. It is important that you bring balance into your various forms of expression. Bring the aspects of physical, mental, emotional being into alignment with the higher aspect of the spirit that you are from within. Listen to your heart and do not dismay over appearances.

✦   ✦

✦

Allow time each day to quiet your mind from any thoughts. Meditate in prayerful oneness with the spirit of divine grace. This state of grace is within you as a part of the great I am. Be of peaceful intent and allow yourself to simply be in this place where you will more readily discover that which calls to you from the heart of your being. Be at peace my child for it is in connecting with divine wisdom that you will be in harmony with the path of your journey.

✦   ✦

✦

The wise ones have imparted sacred truths unto you and only you can choose that which you will bring to the alter of your heart. Open your heart to that which is of God's grace and let all else fall away. Do not live in fear, but in faith that as you call to only God or God's messengers you will be guided forward through love and grace to your highest good.

✦   ✦

✦

Let go of your perceptions and allow your life to unfold for your highest good. Pause each day to be certain you are bringing balance into the various forms of expression of your life. Be of ever present mind that always and in all ways you are indeed capable of creating this balance. Allow time to express yourself creatively and focus on enjoying the privilege and honor of being in physical incarnation. Most do not recognize the gift they have been given; to walk among those you have co-created with. We say unto you, enjoy the opportunity you have been given to learn, grow and share in a new way.

Cherish the time that is given and do not take for granted those who would share life with you through love and grace. Honor them by being patient and understanding when they are in need. That is not to say you should indulge in rooms of antiquity, for where there is no growth, there will be only wilting flowers. Move forward with dignity and honor through the energy of love and compassion regardless of the adversity you are facing, and know that you are never alone in your journey, for we are ever present showering you with love as you walk the pathway of your tempering.

Be of ever present mind that you are capable of living in and of the Light in every moment and in every realm of consciousness that you exist. However, it is up to you to create the discipline within yourselves to accomplish this. We are here to offer a solution to the darkness that prevails here on the Earth plane. Look at this closely and you will become aware that even those of you with the best of intentions are capable of, and do indeed at times allow, some form of negativity to flow from you. Know that this will only feed on you and grow stronger, tearing you and your fellows down.

Your thoughts, words and actions send into the world the energy to substantiate, to acknowledge and support either Light or darkness. Imagine if you will that a single fragment of thought would be the determining factor that tips the scales to Love, joy and enlightenment. We say unto you, which do you choose? Working in the realms of Light carries a responsibility, and the enlightened one in awareness of the Light, of spiritual law, can no longer walk in the shadows of ignorance.

In Love and Light

Whisperings

✦　✦

✦

S. E. Kuenzel (Kenzel)

Made in the USA
Middletown, DE
22 September 2016